RIVERRUN
Alan Baker

Newton-le-Willows

Published in the United Kingdom in 2019
by The Knives Forks And Spoons Press,
51 Pipit Avenue,
Newton-le-Willows,
Merseyside,
WA12 9RG.

ISBN 978-1-912211-21-0

Acknowledgements:

Versions of these poems have appeared in *Stride*.

Supported using public funding by

**ARTS COUNCIL
ENGLAND**

LOTTERY FUNDED

RIVERRUN
"... the smug and silver Trent"

I don't know at what point I became a student of limnology
haunter of water courses, connoisseur of ox-bows
lover of the liminal tinct of an unsurvivable element
we couldn't survive without, but perhaps when I saw
the glittering spectacle, escaping words, channelled and chased
bridged, banked but in the end, unfathomable, and that
although the linmologist may list the geomorphic features
                              or the hydrologic cycle
that doesn't cut it, no, it's the never-ceasingness
the invisibility to which we say Dear Mystery, are you
ever and always only the water, or the fish and fowl
marshland, canal, embankment, a virtuality continuum flowing
past the man-made caves of Nottingham, breweries
cellars, tanneries, dwellings, mecca bingo, and 2/4 twang
of strings in the upstairs room of a pub on Mansfield Road

how to describe a kingfisher
in flight (it was turquoise-green
with a flash of orange-red as it banked
to change direction, etc.) knowing
it was an idea of a kingfisher
that it was part of the brook, the alders
the fish it would catch, the person watching
and now describing, it was colour
and I walk, headphones off
listening to the leaves
speaking in tongues
of the river that lives in every cell
laying claim to the world
and everything in it

wanting whale-calls and the moth-filled
nights of childhood, wanderers
follow the river through flooded delta
whispering ice and the evidence
of a raised beach, mono-culture
marsh and irrigation channels
and rural towns with suspicious lights
meanwhile, a place of refuge exists
in the realm of language
democratic as it is
and full of direct address
familiar forms, shared concepts
and frameworks for envisaging
what might be, or has been

an alternative future populated
by the minnows and sticklebacks
of legend and homely nightmare
dreaming so many parallel paths
augmented angles, google-bugs
of our wartime nostalgia
of willows grating the air
splayed quietly into reflected selves
sung crowsfoot, gurgled chickweed
like a muscle moving diligently
spliced into a main where winds
linger or freshwater betrayals
leave nymphs singing to a demented sky
sticky with promise

all rivers call with the same voice
the same gold and green, the same
blue, bright, yellow surfaces
that are what they seem
opening into colourless waveform
that encourages swift at evening
and bat at temporal twist
into pale pastel, watercolour sketch
so, river, sing me a strangeness
rippling life into whatever
daydream lingers at your surface
you have barges, quays, buoys, saltspray
and difficult horizons, and lend a voice
to those who share your seaward path

sing me some snatch of song, green
and full of the words used to describe antiquity
when it was new as the morning
or how the lichen moulds the tree
every bit as much as the trunks
mould the A6005, ancient way
made new by petrol
write me a spare and ascetic guide
to the ginnels and cul-de-sacs
close to the tobacco factory (site of)
encode it in runes and hexadecimal
and let it lead to architectural space
transparent as sky, the like of which
only the church had given us before

I watch a young woman
walk over the bridge
in the nightlit city, a slender person
walking purposefully, head bowed
and I wonder what chance has in store
and wish her well, so well, in fact
that my wish brings me nearer
to prayer than I've ever been
a prayer to chance
or to the gold-green wavelets
of the streetlit river, to hope
or to whatever goddess watches over
slender, bowed
purposeful young persons

the past is beset
by beautiful dangers
which, according to
the Oxford Dictionary of Regret
are those we avoided, and yet whose colours
lingered long enough for their calamities
to leak into our lives
so, o river, teach us
that every green has its own shade
every sea can be crossed, every man
every woman, the sleek petrel
and the little eel, their own country
they never stick to it, asking of rivers
only that they take them home

salmon-pink invests in real estate
every evening, offering its warmth
to the ring road and suburban trees
picking out details in brick terraces
and high emotions in silent hotel rooms
which offer water under each bridge
and a perfect night's sleep in which salmon
leap upstream to the light
which bears their simile – observe
the dream leans and taps his shoulder
and me, I left there a long time ago
I was a different place, less fertile
indifferent, less homely and loved
in a familiar way, deceptively stable

he's gone to sea
silver buckles on his knee
in which the sea
is some unknown quantity
of time and space, that claims
his songs, his looks, his laughter
his golden curls, his interest
in allotments and the history
of working men's clubs
separated by anxiety
from a world
built out of sentences
he builds it instead
out of broken English

even though age
has sowed white hairs on thee
I still don't believe
that you and I have travelled as far
as even the bend in the river
let it ever recede that bend, hidden by trees
that oxbow lake, that white-water
with speed limits, poor visibility
and an unknown script telling its story
as glowworms and bats
glide into consciousness
seeds of summer grasses
are new worlds opening
into tiny epics

looking out over herb-rich pasture
young trees, the soulful eyes
of women at the well
herdsmen, dog-walkers, bin men
encampments with a column of smoke
it may seem that commodification
of History had occurred
were it not for the glistening sycamores'
young leaves, in which a beginning
was evident, waveform, fructiform
fractal intelligence of ox-bow
and meander, and over wave-sound
harebells rang on the moor
miles away, but I heard them

lack of light
sees stars
bright as anything
over church tower tilting
towards the Trent
swollen from melt
as the times amble
into deeper dark sucked
into a skyscape scored
by ash branches
particular crystals
reconnect all network drives
in clockwork wavelets
welcoming migrants into night

co-terminus with the events themselves
is the anticipation of their loss
so says the wise man
watching canada geese graze
on the far meadow, flooded
in part, the water dazzling
in the low winter sun, the geese
beautiful, anonymous, non
human (how can they bear the cold?)
classless and colourless
with vocal apparatus able to construct
the most human of cries
in which the meanings are unstable
and I can make whatever I want seem true

given a river's silver sleeve
and living vein, then we may have music
gatherings on the quay
multiple discourses
struck copper, sparks and cries
of hawkers, skein and skylight
and the bobbed wave's weight
as a barge goes by
arranged rock
and meadow, subterranean terraces
streams gone down
to craftsmen's caves
garrulous silences
and spoken wave

under our dreams the river
behind our eyes, emerging
from culvert, ditch, storm-drain
overhang and silt, current
and tidal-bore, lisps boundaries as if
nothing is easier than erosion or division
prototype frontier, original sign
of no entry, give us inspiration
amnesia, promises
and while you're at it yield up the souls
of the psychotic, the depressed
the simply desperate
the unutterably sad
we know they're dissolved in your urban soup

surely this river is some kind of metaphor!
somewhere, as it circles Nottingham
its currents conceal the lost lanes of Narrow Marsh
the lament of Reform Act rioters
hanged in the market square
the rattle of the loom
in the hungry alleys
its narrows elide
the formulae of George Green
the paradigm of every self-taught mathematician
and mill-boy, whispering his equations
to perch and pike, freshwater crayfish
the infrequent otter, while the river
basks in the sun

alder, willow, duckweed, all
expect the call of ferrymen
fishermen, boatmen, bargemen
a world of men, listening to her ripples
her silent verbs of movement
metamorphosis, airless depths
murk and sunlit beauty
she accepts the world, but realises
it may be replaced by a dream
of the world, awoken today, the day
she was born, where she's lived
all her life, Moonday morning, day
of insomnia, of the mayflies'
single day of life

river as liminal interface
between elements incompatible
but relying on each other
for all earthly needs
as air and water, earth bank
frog-stabbing heron
pike that take a duckling
fertility of flood, seasonal
sun and air shaping course
attrition exposing, unearthing
as if the world might be the sum
of all the people not limited
to the field of vision
or the songs used to celebrate it

dipping the oars of an eight-person scull
all the body to heave and push
I remember the weight, water
resisting like a live thing
as it was when it lived
under the Barton ferry, that craft
of legend, edgeways word
in the story of this world
the call-and-response of canada geese
snipe and black-headed gull
luring the unwary to the river-border
the oarsman our only hope of crossing
from lacklustre life to the other side
resisting like a live thing, sadly mistaken

bulrushes, reeds, bric-a-brac, lack
of foothold in the marl
deposits centuries old
displacement on a grand scale
enticement to drunks, lure
to anglers, how can
a river be owned? it moves
and does not move, never stops
to let anyone out
lean enemy of flight
is how she might be described
or an inducement to it
to hunger after that green country
over the bridgeless, ferryless flood

sucked into cooling towers
strange dignity, sulphur dioxide
turned into TV images, black night river
the blue-grey day river does the river
still exist when it's distilled, looking back
on itself, boundless above the
creeping estates and landfills
refractions singularly distanced
from galleries of migrating swallows
we have lingered in the channels
of freshwater ecology
and seen it contaminated by runoff
the cormorant, enemy to anglers
hanging its wings in mourning

a river's green beginnings
heat-haze over leaf-shade
gathered thunder
and singing birds existing
as a fluctuating population
lost in a place where reedbeds lean
and the wind has a stranger note
as if the blue was more
than refracted light and the breeze
wasn't a melody borrowed
from lone individuals blown far outside
their customary ranges
to interchange of world and world
(twilight watches the surface change)

she wanders lowlands
where the privilege of morning
is not too bright or sudden
nor grey and inarticulate
she speaks of troubles
and the need for comfort
in the overlap between the real
and the imaginary
the mind's place, not to be changed
increasingly encroaching on the physical
land green and she is free to roam
the pollen-filled air, the roots of trees
with lovers, lying like them
in liquid vowels that don't say what they mean

today, tea, black and strong
to the rescue, as a working day
revolves on an instant message
or being prodded by an electronic
device, ululate call and lap of shoreline
listing as it slips into a new element
always changing, an excess
a lack of restraint
a lifetime re-lived each season
obsessively drawn to its own concerns
as the desperate are, as all those
carried by water they know not where
from looking on bullet-holed walls
only the river reconstructed

the river is paleolithic, the river
is our fate, its unstoppability, it is
cardio-vascular, muscular
the wrestling with the love of the good
life and plastic in the duckweed, irony
in the frogspawn, simulacrum and spirit-guide
of sand martin and dipper, the river
is ornithology, our connection
to algae and millstone grit, and
as sediments bury cities and filters
sift folk-lore to oblivion, we refuse
to stop interfering, or interfere too little
adapted as we are to highways
and evolved to spot a bargain

all night the river strikes notes
that blur to one note
now interrupted by the wind
now fighting back in music
all its own, while the lonely
have their own words
snatched, or repeated, half
-remembered, the river is solitary
never stopping, always another
desolate promontory
some rapids, exhausting
to travel alone, like the trickster god
haunter of housing estates
recycling plants, the job centre

one wonders whether wetlands
will still wind their streams
allow wading birds and wintering
migrants sanctuary and shelter
or whether storm surges and saline levels
inundation and erosion
will erase their traces
we want levels of collective memory
to deepen, we want bee colonies
to thrive, enlightenment to take hold
lucky people to walk their dogs
by the river, red post office vans
to go from door to door
under a biographical sky

gypsum and millstone grit

carboniferous coal measures

marls and seams

triassic sherwood sandstone

mercia mudstone (distinctive red coloured strata)

permian lower magnesian limestone

carboniferous limestone

sand, gravels and alluvium deposits

Burton Ale, Nottinghamshire coal

D H Lawrence flying pickets Wollaton Hall

the cellars and labyrinths carved

under Nottingham, haulage

by canal and rail, warehouses

and Nottingham lace

the eyes are filled, variable, green
and beauty is in them, the trees
murmur as green as the world
easy to sit still, easy as being
where we are
and nowhere else
it's that simple, except the river
never stops, and morning steps
into the room unembarrassed
with an open mind
to take us by barge, narrow-boat
or whatever means, but onwards
please simplify my life, river
it's the least you can do for me

the night doesn't belong to lovers
it belongs to our dreams, and they
may love us or hate us, it's hard
to say, though some say the night
belongs to the river, it shares
its depth, its cool, its propensity
to overwhelm us, it is the dark
side of the planet, though others say
that underpinning its deployment
requires gravel bed configuration
risk management, early warnings
fast-flowing melt-water and shallows
to reflect the sunlight of another age
the echo of its thunder, its tears of pollen

on the surface a uniform grey
but in the depths an inner life
boundless and bright
swept by horizons
tight as buds opening to the possible
as if to say think of a world
and the world exists
and Heraclitus just can't keep up
because at times everything seems
close and small, usually at night
wondering how far the flood-plain extends
and whether it's better to be
in the world, or of the world
when frogs are invading the kitchen

something is changing, something
may be unstoppable
and it is involved in larger forces
levels of ice and sea, complexity
of speech and act, in a garden
or kitchen, or the unreeling of sleep
the moth at evening, the fly by day
the witless universe on roller skates
on a moped, through sniper's alley
postal-code gangland tracks
food banks, something is changing
and all the king's horses
and all the king's men
are being deployed in case of insurrection

and today the river is an eye
inward and specialised
peering into sand-martin burrows
winking to the lonely fisherman
fixing him with a stare, today
the river is an I, self-absorbed
and intent on grasping the moment
of departure, though it never departs
constructing its own landscape
from overhang and silt, trilling
out of necessity, to prevent
flood and drought, or at least
to smear them both
with the tantalising gleam of another world

black branches against a white sky
and the questions stands
what does our machine amount to?
food, sleep, sex and sometimes
song, black branches over white
water, weir, untrammeled, free
among the unhoused birds
drinking tea, the river's gleam
the whole green and silver mass
words in air, I didn't expect
the waters to be this cold
or the birds on the wire
to be so numerous or the ways
in which they awakened something in me so multiple

take me to the river, show me that river
by the river we sat down and wept
I went down to the river, I was born
by the river, riverrun past Adam
and Eve river, moon river, down by
the river side, cry me a river
when the slatted rectangle of incendiary delight
which is morning speaks silently
of the hours to come, coffee locks
onto the nervous system, colours
invade the room, yellow-white
green, and the river's blue-grey
is a reminder of distance, somewhere
we can't get to, or that we don't want others to get to

the bridge steps up to the river, then stops
being a remnant only
of the Middle Ages
and having a chapel over it
as was common then (but not now)
you get used to the gap
eventually, it's just the river
in everyday rain reflecting the bridge
travelers, bells at dusk
the dome of the sky and the homeless in the streets
shallows and mud flats
belie the life below the surface
of language and custom, if we're pilgrims
then we're all the same

crystallography tells us
about the transformation of water
in the shallows and reed-beds
into something slower
brittle and white, like land, the interior
even more mysterious
glitter, scud of ducks slithering
embryonic glacier or reminder of what's lost
wrapped in the silver warmth of the ice
imaginary swallows dream the sands and dunes
of an African south under
grey-blue-steel-cloud-moon-black-white river
hey river! why so pedestrian?
swallower of dreams, what is it with you?

when it rises in heather and spagnum moss
it is potential, prototype of Hotspur
and Heraclitus, their ideas of a river
synchronising ripples, adverbs
waterfall, cymbal crash, babble
of books in brooks, dipper and king
-fisher haunted whirl and eddy
ripple, splash, backflow, drag, current
and swell into calm
of spawn and newt country
washerwoman world of linen dirt streamed
black-and-blue rumours, always aware
of flood risk, toxicity levels,
scarcity of native species

on days of algal bloom and looming skies
the river assumes a name, as if names
ignored frontiers, as if it wasn't
a north/south paradigm
a border between us and other
where vowels stiffen, inflections fall away
glacial melt, is it? the stink of mink?
banked and broadened
struggling like a live thing
with migration
summer arrivals
patterns of drought and swell
levels of diversity
and language acquisition

repeated low-pressure systems
from the Atlantic basin
cross and re-cross
the midlands plain
water-logged catchment, snow-melt
becoming memory
of legendary flood
its narrative possibilities
which give us the Trent
magically alive in the sense
that magic is transformation
of sand martin nests
to living riverbanks
calling the faithful each spring

waiting to be filled by spring, fracked by June
bladed clouds bringing narratives
on the lip of flood, edge of drought
Severn-Trent catchment
sky pale blue, the alders black and brown
the water doesn't have its own colour
but contributes movement
through straw-yellow fields, almost colourless
glandular landscape only enlivened by the winking red
of Radcliffe power station reflected in the water
pesticide levels, sewage and cyanide,
hydraulic fracturing, gravel extraction
(am I more afraid of the words used
to describe the river than of the river itself?)

the river talks, eventually
to everyone, the tone of voice
is bardic, fit for miracles
nuanced by patches of yellow
faded grass, by walkers carving the air
with their anecdotes and laughter
(the absence of an "I" lightening their tone
and they in turn lightening the river)
who needs these grand narratives?
(except in dreams
or the waking dream of insomnia)
I realised that the river had entered my psyche
when I dreamt it lapped the door
of my house, a good mile from its banks

it was known for changing its course
on the midlands plain, bends became lakes
overhangs silt, what was once a meadow
became a world of aquatic creatures, pond-weed
murk, and the sounds are distant sounds
of a remembered childhood or species long gone
(curlew, corncrake, great crested newt) and new
frontiers, policed, that don't accept
the stamp on your passport
that don't offer a way to cross the flood
even though that land was once yours, and now
different language and customs
dangerous sand-banks and currents not to be
trifled with, and the river is a border

drivers on the M1 risked lives
to gawk at the mile-wide river
in spate, enlarging its vocabulary
getting above itself, shining like an inland sea
a shifting border, arbitrary, lacking certainty
and those meadows, rye grass and fescue
wet and shining in the winter sun, busy
with machinery, drilling, fracturing, and no-one
is allowed to stop them, we're not citizens
of that place, and it's 4.30am, clouds
cover the moon, and the river is an emptiness
an absence, invisible, and I'm a worried employee
who can't sleep and keeps thinking about the Trent
my mutable, silent, ultimately unreliable frontier

slung lines taut, blue blush
of winter's kiss, blasted
seemingly immortal, pulverized
steamed, driven into drains, culverts
liquidity ratios, plash mode
who wouldn't be angry when
misrule and rebelliousness
in unequal measure met George Beck
aged 20, boatman, hanged
in Nottingham market square
Wednesday 1st February 1832
ferried from shore, for ever lost
young boatman, sampling the dark
depths (let that be a lesson to others)

rather than looking at the rippled grey expanse
straining to see gradations, its levels
(swollen in March), hidden warblers
among the leafless willows
wouldn't it be better to imagine it?
then its depths, peopled and at play
can illuminate the stories you tell of it
(how a kingfisher who is the river
factors refraction into its gaze
becomes the fish) or how barges
with coal, slow-drawn, sepia, silt
and the soils of every country 'twixt here and there
part its surface like the old ferryman
no ghost, alive as you and me

from bream and barbel, pike and gudgeon
chub, perch, roach and rudd we glean
a fishy taxonomy we can weave
into our own words, a classification
of ponds and wetlands, drumlins and alluvial clay
the Severn-Trent catchment serving
seven million people, land of midland surburbia
where Heraclitus and Lord Byron argue the toss
in the Barton Ferry, "though the waters
are always changing, the river stays the same"
says H, though the other demurs
saying the river has wrong-footed him
and that noon sits under his eyelids
painting an ideal world in coloured ink

what do I owe this moving mirror
(never reflecting the same thing twice)
continuum of hope, from yesterday
to the angst of tomorrow?
I owe it frogspawn and water-boatmen
the art of meditation, murmurations
on autumn evenings, fricative, inflexion
an elongated vowel zone, demilitarised
and multi-lingual, existing
by liquid grammar and paradox
said the light, glancing twice
at the ridge-and-furrow fields
where, each autumn, mist settles
and the river is more than metaphor

am I repeating myself out of desperate hope?
or is the river habit-forming?
when did I know that it would keep me
against my will? I think it was
when I no longer needed to look at the river
to write about its blues and greys
its surface patterns or the shapes it carves
in the alluvial soil - it became my inner landscape
I moved with its moods, dissolved into its surroundings
its waterlogged fields, subsuming myself
into its local inflections and the habits of thought
moulded by the river's turn of phrase
I'll always be an outsider, I know, but the river
loves outsiders, even as it keeps them from their home

these poems Dear Reader are trying
in fourteen-line units to contain
immensities (and the rain-filled river is getting
more immense as I write)
as if in words I could make the smug and silver Trent
run in a new channel, fair and evenly
not cut off from so rich a bottom here, not
come cranking in to drown
a zone of golden pollen
free to drift among vocabularies
when the rain stops and the broad stream
with its muscular grip restrains
the Atlantic clouds and grey skies
and lets slip a sunny spell to welcome wanderers

the kingfisher and the bat at eve
the natterjack toad and the great crested newt
the willow warbler and dipper keep their green
and muddy worlds out of sight, marginal
married to the glamour of the ghost-river
the dream-river, river of copious rain
surrounder of everything, which comes
when we least expect it
groggy remembrance freshly-ground
coffee in the morning fails to chase
illicit bliss, nostalgia stalking water-meadows
walking where wing-mirrors won't see us
riverward, on the rive gauche stocked
with artists' views and sermons in stones

I no longer remember
exactly when it was that the river
and I became one,
perhaps it was when
my vocal chords gave birth
to shallows and sand-banks
to gradations of blue
and my skin grew cold to the touch
and friends said
I was going nowhere
(the Trent never reaches the sea)
or maybe it was when
my language became
incomprehensible to my own ears

twenty-five million years ago, fish
developed their communal habits
social behaviour, their "language"
us, we've only just arrived!
birds of passage, waxwing and fieldfare
sandpiper, pink footed goose, swallows from Africa
strange languages, indefinite detention, visas
the river welcomes them all, opens its floodplain
fertile, shining, green, but prone to flood and treacherous
because to live near a river is to be bounded
by a cruel reflection of the sky
you have to go many miles to get round it
(they're building a new bridge
it's for high speed trains, not you and I)

I went down to the river
for healing and renewal
and the dream of making sense
and wet grass and mud
calmed me with the memory
of those who've crossed before us
and the river reminded me
of a friend, spoke to me
with colours of spring
but I also remembered that it's deaf
unaware of its own strength or of
its eye of newt, leg of frog
fish-scale glitter, gills
it isn't human, it doesn't care about us

with my compact binoculars (8 x 21)
I can see a mink, ravenous predator
stalking water voles and rabbits
moving sap and gum
of greening trees
seeps into some kind
of spring-time urge
even when you want to be left
alone not reminded
about inhabiting a green shade
or waiting for the flood
to claim you as an undiscovered country
the mink is imaginary
only if our thoughts are imaginary

clouds carpet vistas steel
concrete cooling wind sulphur
dioxide warming the valley
empire piled northern coal
cotton lace bicycles beer
central heating and making sure
the lights don't go out
tonight at dusk, the fields brown
brown the weight of water
under brown skies
I've seen sand martin nests
submerged in summer flood
but at least your shoals are abundant
and you provide gravel for the construction industry

from the river to St. Ann's Well
and Radford Road
always a boundary
when enclosure came
later the loom-breakers
radical bookshops
old stories of picket lines and pensions
funded by scratch cards and lottery tickets
and the Trent had freedom to roam
gathered and guided
a tapestrie of May-month meadows
as if we could all fleet the time carelessly
through the river's industry a golden age
maybe it will come again

beyond the cluster of bare trees
there are allotments, and beyond those
the winter sun lights a brick terrace
parallel to others, and I think that
tenacity is what's required, or fatalism
in the face of business parks and
the global knowledge economy
while the river reminds us
that it's a city of reflections
that the engine of our days is idling
the water of our wetlands
is increasingly saline, and a memory leak
is fuelling the currents and undertows
that drag us to unmentionable places

each morning mist
rises from the Trent
simple transformation
from bud to leaf
leaves me cellular
leaves me sadness
that the river is more than metaphor
that it is getting serious
said the west wind piling
clouds from Radcliffe power station
before beginning with a story
in which you become your own reflection
lady of the valley and the waving wheat
it's you that I turn to

pontoon jetties, white water
for kayaks and canoes, nine
sprint lanes, words can't come
fast enough for this triathlon-friendly
world of water though what
would the Barton ferryman think, shady
disreputable, working after dark
when the weary traveler has no choice
when she blends with the browns and greys
feels the current's drag, the tug of weed
submerged bike-chains and shopping carts
hallucinates underwater worlds
and wishes the Trent would run in a new course
evenly, and fair

where is Nottingham's river?
it's under the ring-road flyover
or meandering out of town
through urban-blight fields
it has no mouth or delta
no loud falls or famous wharves
just a Midland Water Company warehouse
and a ferry no-one ever sees
with no important destination
only stability (that "underpinned industries
and arable production")
hydrology dictating erosion and deposition
and I've had enough of its silences
and enigmatic moods

I thought I'd written the river
constructed its plot-twists
composed its songs, its pathetic fallacies
I thought it was my invention
magnificent and brooding, skipping in summer
I thought I knew it, but now I understand
that it was the river that invented me
I'm one of its characters, especially at night
when it drenches my sleep in water-cress and mint
dreams me into the one morning of the year
when the May-flies rise in the sun
takes me into their swarms, into the swallows'
patternings and the animations of starlings
greets me with the timely intervention of renewal

Lightning Source UK Ltd.
Milton Keynes UK
UKHW040618291019

352508UK00001B/65/P